Coral Gardens

PATRICIA GLEICHAUF

Illustrated by Karen Staszko

Coral Gardens

Copyright © 2020 Patricia Gleichauf
Second Edition

Published by Legacy Key Press

All rights reserved

No part of this publication may be reproduced, distributed, or transmitted in any form or by any means, including photocopying, recording, or other electronic or mechanical methods, without the prior written permission of the publisher, except in the case of brief quotations embodied in reviews and certain other noncommercial uses permitted by copyright law.

The moral right of the author has been asserted.

Originally published by Page Publishing 2020

ISBN 979-8-9895453-9-1 (paperback)
ISBN 979-8-9911726-0-8 (hard cover)
ISBN 979-8-9911726-1-5 (digital)

Library of Congress Control Number: 2024915064

Printed in the United States of America

To Maddie: my shoe and jewelry girl.
Always keep your sparkle!

XOXO

Backyard gardens are as pretty as can be.

But nothing can compare
to the gardens in the sea.

Coral reefs are ocean gardens,
each has a dazzling hue.
They are home to many sea animals
and many sea plants too.

Long thought to be plants with colorful, swaying tentacles, coral was later discovered to be a tiny saltwater animal.

A single coral animal is called a polyp.
It looks like a sea anemone.

Baby coral are called larva. They can swim in salt water freely.

Coral babies drift in the ocean until they find a place to attach.

Rocks formations and old coral reefs are a very good match.

Once rooted, each larva baby grows into a polyp of hard or soft coral. Hard polyps are reef-building coral. They are rigid and stony and stand in one place.

Soft coral polyps attach to a coral reef or the ocean floor. They are flexible and can move within their space.

Hard coral polyps build a bony skeleton around themselves using ocean minerals. They divide again and again to become colonies of salt water animals.

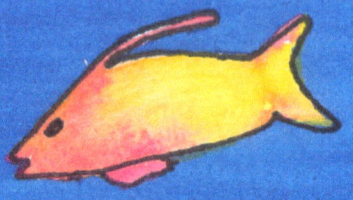

Hard Corals

Elkhorn

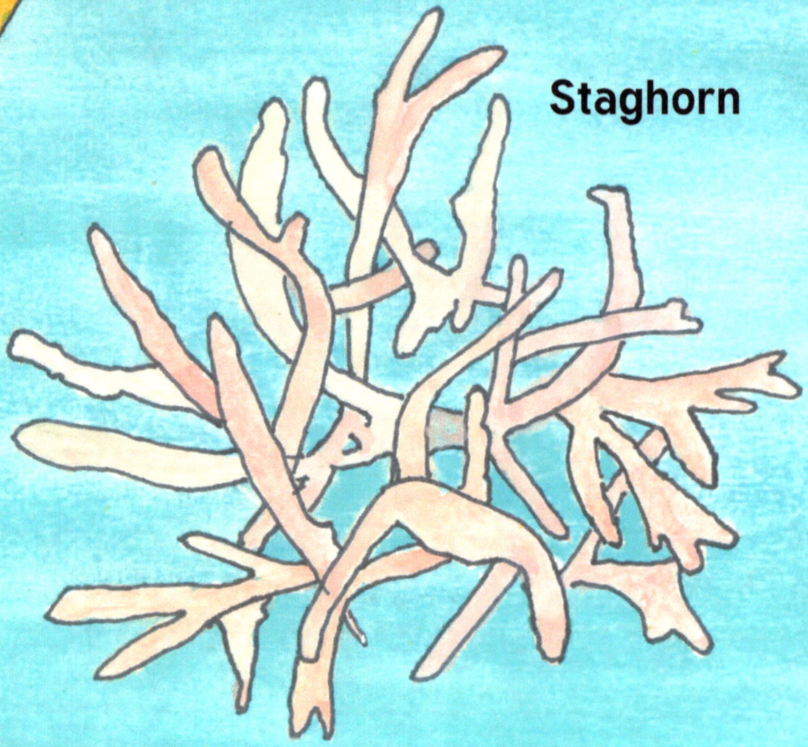

Staghorn

Brain

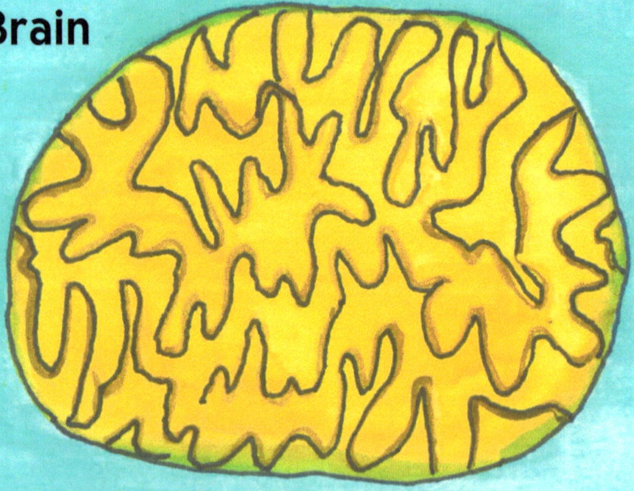

There are hundreds of types of coral. It is a very long list.

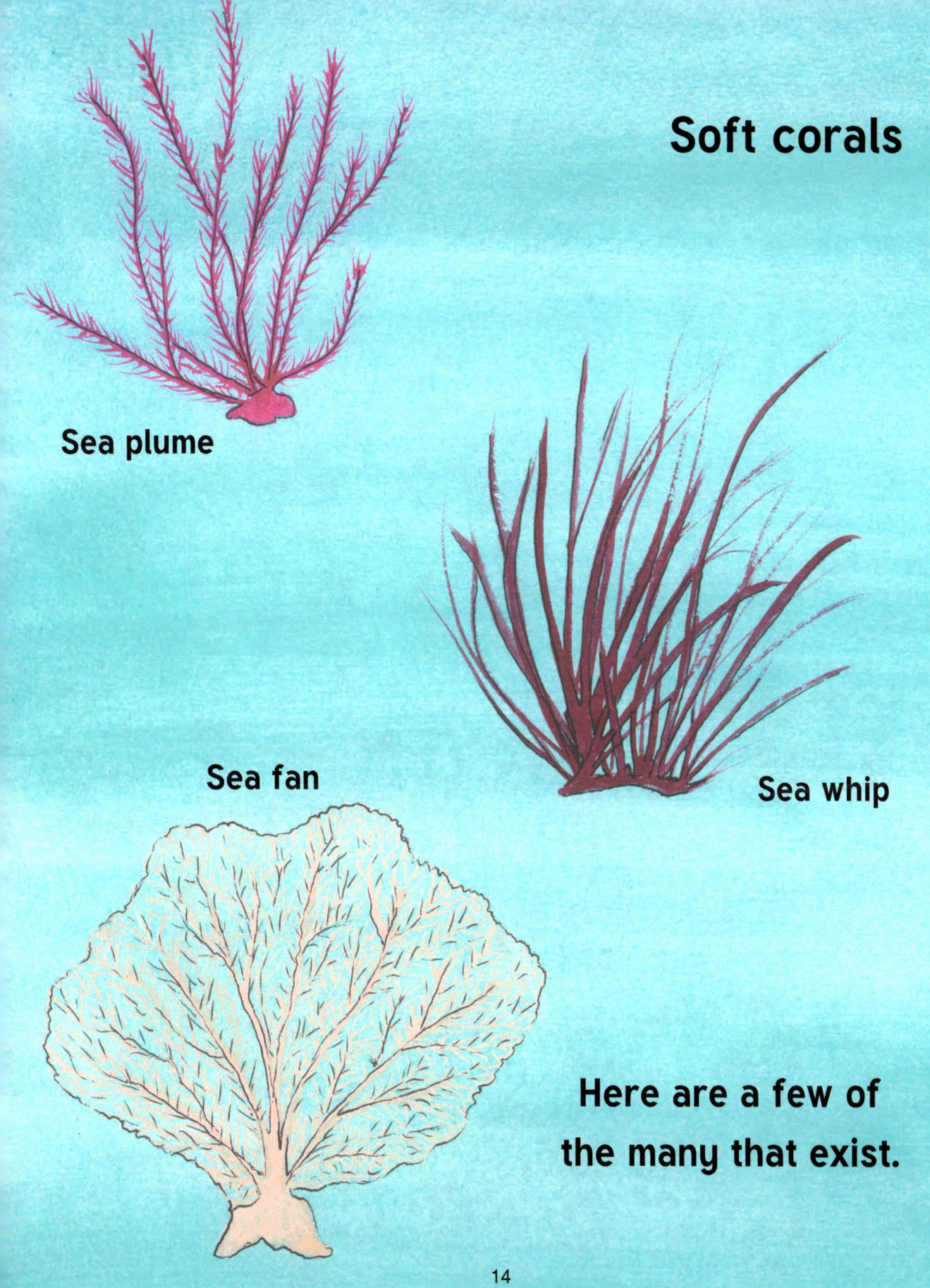

A coral reef is a haven for many sea creatures. They live together, sharing their own special features.

Algae lives inside coral. It uses sunlight to make food that coral needs to live.

Lodging and food for algae is what the coral can give.

Parrot fish and surgeonfish
keep reef algae trimmed.
Sea urchins take over when
they go for a swim.

The water in the reef must be kept sparkling clean. It cannot be murky or gray. Sponges, clams, and sea squirts clean millions of gallons of water every single day!

Predators search coral reefs for
smaller fish on which to feed.
Lion fish, lobster, and sharks lurk in the seaweed.

Cardinal fish and squirrel fish hide in the reef during daylight hours. They come out to feed at night.

Damsel fish and parrot fish hide in the reef when it is dark. They come out to feed when it is light.

Coral reefs create beautiful beaches. Strong ocean waves pound old coral into a fine powdery sand.

Abundant food draws herons, gulls and shorebirds to this tropical land.

Coral reefs need warm, shallow, salt water, and strong sunlight in order to thrive.

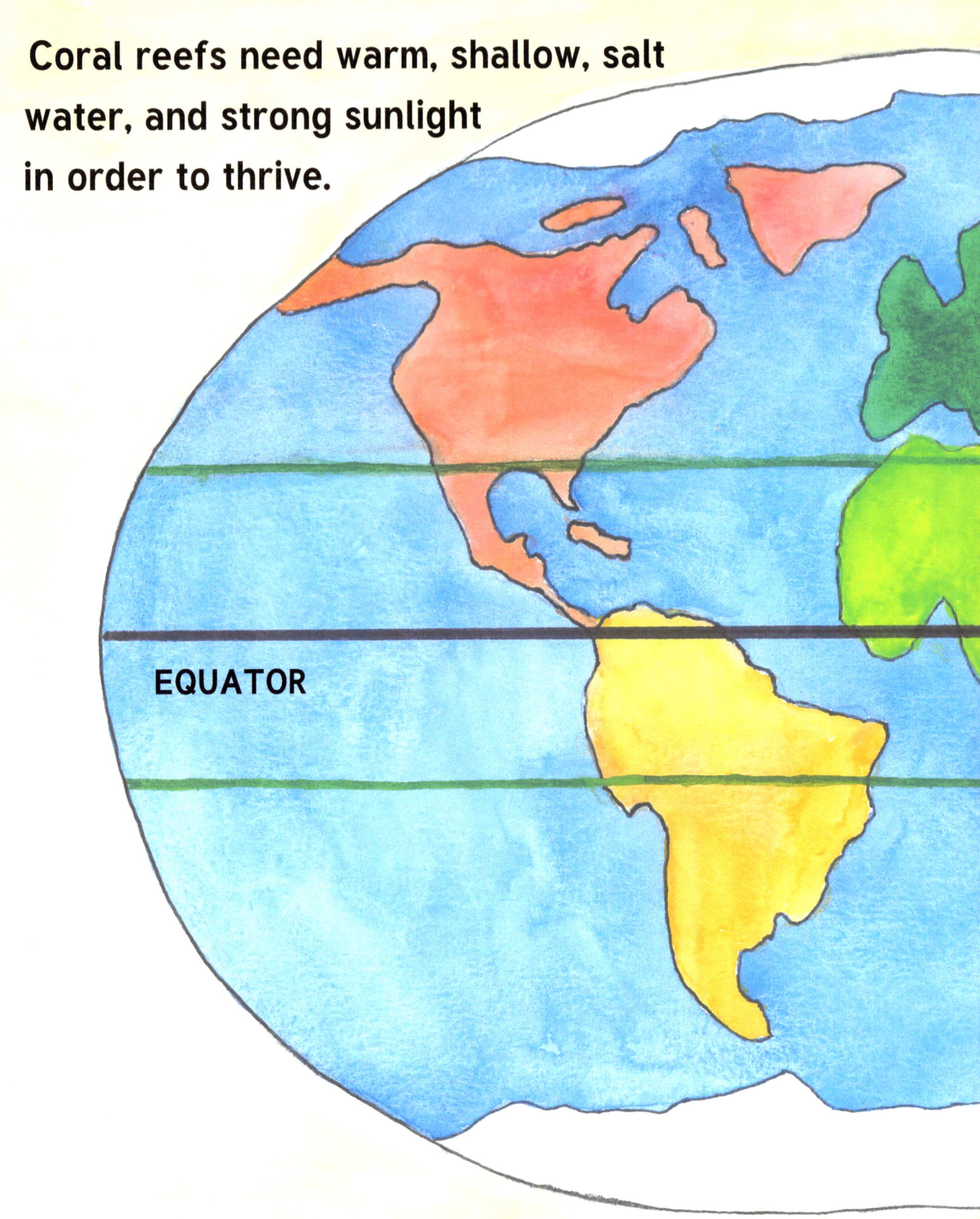

EQUATOR

They are found in a band around the middle of the earth. Near the equator is the only place they can survive.

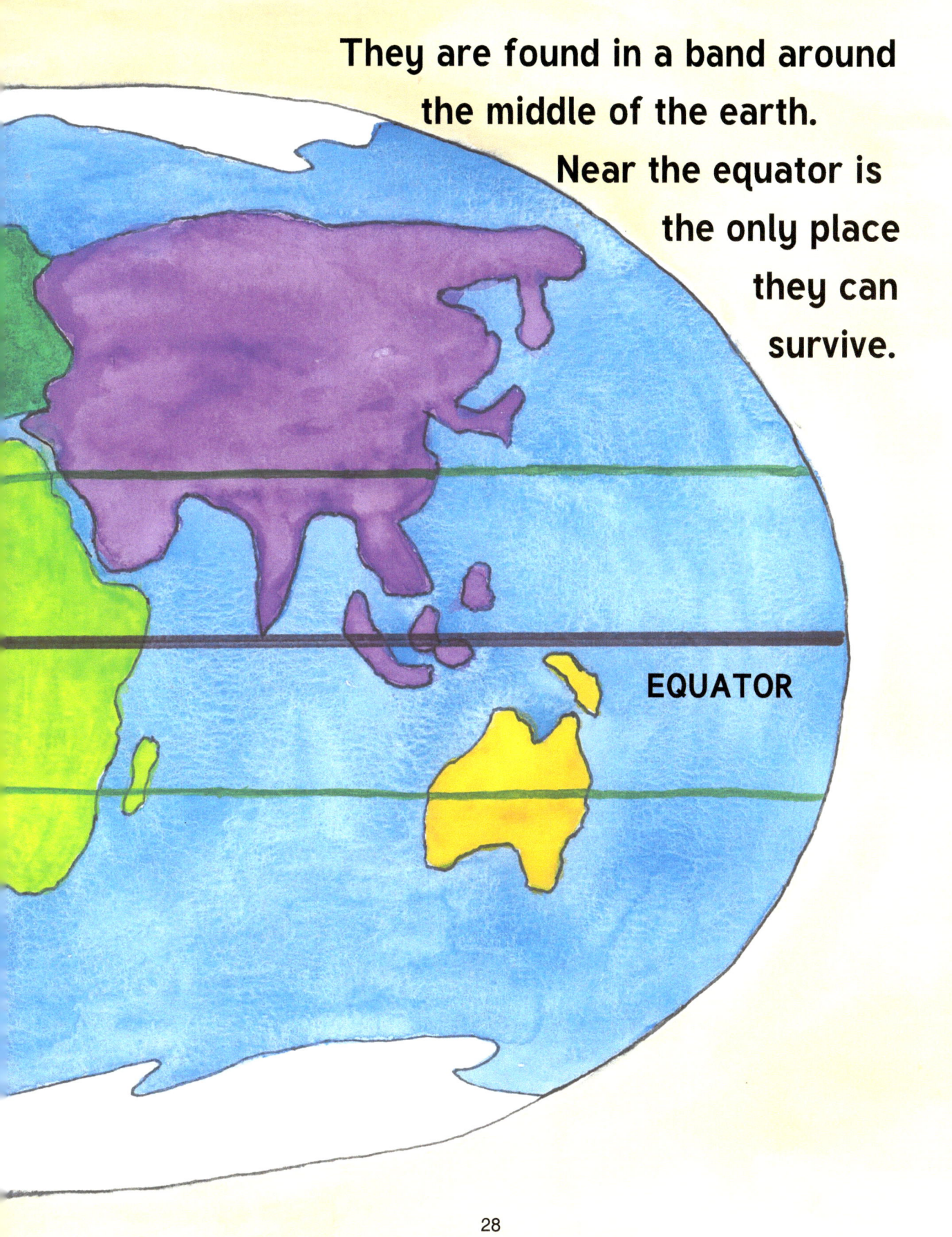

EQUATOR

A coral reef extends as far as your eye can see. It provides a home, food and safety to our ocean family.

This is the fourth book in Patricia Gleichauf's award-winning *Under the Sea* series. Her books became an immediate success and have received the following honors:

Horses of the Sea was awarded a gold medal in the Florida Authors and Publishers Presidential Awards for excellence in children's literature in 2018.

Starfish Gazing was awarded second place in the 2019 International Purple Dragonfly Children's Book Competition, category Picture Books 5 and younger.

Sea Turtles Circle achieved a five-star Readers Favorite review in 2020; finalist status in the Children's books category of the 2020 Eric Hoffer International Book Competition; second place and honorable mention in the 2020 International Purple Dragonfly Children's Book Competition (Picture Books ages 6 and older and ages 5 and younger, respectively); and award winning finalist in the Children's Picture Book: Hardcover Non-Fiction category of the 2020 International Book Awards.

The entire *Under the Sea* series was awarded a bronze medal in the International Moonbeam Children's Book Competition in 2019.

About the Author

Pat Gleichauf lives in Upstate New York with her husband, Jack. Writing for children is her dream come true. She is dedicated to children's literacy, and her goal is to "hook kids on books." Pat doesn't miss an opportunity to read her books to students at schools and libraries. She uses this time to encourage children to follow their dreams.

About the Illustrator

Karen Staszko has been creating beautiful watercolor paintings for the past thirty years. She studied watercolor painting for seventeen years and has been teaching it for eleven years. Karen and her husband, Meron, are now living in North Ridgeville, Ohio, to be closer to their daughter and grandson. They lived for eleven years in Southwest Florida. Karen loves art in any form. Her passion is teaching art.

www.ingramcontent.com/pod-product-compliance
Lightning Source LLC
Chambersburg PA
CBHW061157030426
42337CB00002B/30